Milky Green

PHALAENOPSIS CARE FOR BEGINNERS:

Everything You Need to Know About Moth Orchids Gardening, How to Water Phalaenopsis orchids, Orchid Fertilizing, Easy and Long-lasting Blooming, Re-potting, and more

Milky Green

" Phalaenopsis Care for Beginners: Everything You Need to Know About Moth Orchids Gardening, How to Water Phalaenopsis orchids, Orchid Fertilizing, Easy and Long-lasting Blooming, Re-potting, and more"

Dedicated to my grandmother.

Thank you for teaching me to love animals and plants like people!

Re Potted in Sept. 2024

Contents

INTRODUCTION

Why growing Phalaenopsis orchids

*P*halaenopsis orchids are amazingly beautiful flowers! Although they do not produce intoxicating aromas, they are still one of the most beloved types of plants nowadays. In recent years, orchids (especially the Phalaenopsis type, also called moth orchid) are a preferred gift for any occasion!

But why the sudden popularity of this plant family? My answer is the beautiful and long-lasting blooms. Not many plants can produce flowers for more than several days to give you joy and satisfaction and to make your home feel cozier and look more elegant.

No wonder orchids can often be found in the homes of the affluent people and high-class hotels and SPA centers. There is something magnetic and mystical about these plants that attracts our attention and affection.

Unfortunately, many people feel discouraged about growing orchids. As it seems, this is not such a straight-forward and easy process as it may look at first. That is why I decided to share my insights on growing Phalaenopsis orchids. Because being a novice and not a very good plant caretaker in general, I made many rookie mistakes I want to prevent you from repeating.

Reading different, often controversial, manuals didn't help since I felt more confused and discouraged, rather than educated and confident.

As a result, my first orchid was not growing very well – the leaves were limp, the new ones were growing smaller and most importantly – it was not blooming year after year.

But finally, I found the magic sauce! After more and more self-education and experimenting, I finally decoded my Phalaenopsis! I created my own schedule for watering, fertilizing, re-potting, etc. and all the efforts paid off handsomely! Now I enjoy the magnificent blooms of this tropical plant for months which gives me lots of satisfaction and a sense of pride.

So, I decided to share my experience with everyone, just like me, who is confused and unable to get things right. I will be as detailed and practical as possible! No general talk, no fluff!

THE CORRECT
PLACEMENT

What should we do right after we get our Phalaenopsis orchid (or any other type of orchid)? You probably received this plant as a gift (Phalaenopsis is a very popular gift idea for Mother's Day, St. Valentine's Day, International Women's Day, etc.), or maybe you bought it yourself.

Don't have an orchid yet? No worries, in this article I have created the ultimate to-buy list for all orchid fans — from getting your first Phalaenopsis orchid to propagating and taking care of it in the best possible way (in my opinion, of course)! Go to **https://bit.ly/2DB7rvb** or scan the QR code:

The point is that the plant is currently blooming — that's how they are usually sold or they won't be very attractive for purchasing. So, these are my recommendations on how to start your orchid care right from the start, so it continues to bloom for a longer period, and more importantly — the plant stays healthy and vibrant for the next blooming season!

Where to place your orchid?

This is an extremely important part of growing orchids because it determines the amount of light the plant receives. If it is overexposed to direct sunlight, it might burn and dry out. On the flip side – with not enough light it will grow weak and may not be able to produce flowers.

To find out their best placement in your house, we need to take a look at their natural habitat – the jungles and rainforests.

In the wild, the Phalaenopsis plant is growing on large trees under their crowns in partially shady, partially sunny places. So, we need to emulate this placement as much as possible.

In other words, your orchid must be put on a spot with enough light but it should not be direct sunlight, or the amount of direct sunlight is limited during the day.

A common problem with orchids is overexposing them to strong sunlight and burning them rather quickly. This is because it has been said over and over again that they love sunlight, but we often forget that too much of it can kill them easily. Remember that orchids are very durable and sturdy – they are unique for their ability to photosynthesize through their root system as well. So, your plant will be able to gather all the light it needs pretty much from every spot as long as you do not burn it.

Here are some examples:

Eastern, western, and northern windows are perfect but you still have to check how the plant reacts. The eastern window on the top floor of an apartment building will get more hours of sunlight compared to the one at the bottom floor shaded by nearby buildings. Also, the same placement will get you different results during the different seasons and different countries as well – it is logical that the intensity of the sun rays is different in Canada compared to Texas.

You get the point – the best way to determine whether the spot is suitable is to take good care of the orchid and to frequently check whether the leaves are getting yellow and drying out quickly. That's a sign that it receives too much direct sunlight which is burning the plant.

Southern windows can be suitable as long as the direct sunlight is filtered (especially during summer). You can achieve this by placing some gentle blinds or putting the orchid in a spot away from the window (for instance, the window behind the balcony – this way the sun rays do not fall directly on the plant).

On the other hand, in case your environment is too dark for the majority of the day, you can purchase a simple flower light which will boost the photosynthesis of your orchid and its growth!

Important note*: it is best to keep your plant away from strong direct air drafts well (cold or hot), including air conditioners and heaters. Also, make sure there is not anything in proximity which emits gas fumes of any kind, including fruits which naturally produce ethylene as they ripen. You will find more information on this topic in the chapter on blooming and bud blasts.*

Wherever you decide to place your Phalaenopsis remember to monitor it regularly. If you are watering and fertilizing the plant properly but its leaves start getting soft, limpy, yellow and dry, consider moving the plant to a different spot with less light.

Also, do not forget that you can acquire a special plant stand to place several flowers in a small area and save some space. This is an excellent option if your window sills are not available or if there is too much direct sunlight coming through them. By using a stand, you can easily move around the orchids and see how they react to their new environment. There are also some great wall or ceiling hangers you can use to fixate your plants where they feel comfortable, and you basically eliminate the risk of them toppling over to the ground.

Another great option for preventing any unfortunate falls of the pot is by placing the plastic pots inside larger ceramic ones. This setup is very useful when the simple plastic pot is small and the medium is sparse. This makes the container very light which often times cannot sustain a larger plant with a bigger crown. This solution is best for well-established plants with lots of leaves. This way the flower would not need to use the roots inside the planter for photosynthesis that much. By placing it inside a ceramic pot you not only add more aesthetics to your environment, but it also creates more stability for the orchid as well. Just remember that the roots inside need to be well aerated. So, pick a large enough ceramic container to create more free space for the roots to be ventilated. If you need to check on the root system, you just lift the plastic pot, and voila! This option is also very nifty and practical for the watering and fertilizing of the plant. We can just pour the liquid in the ceramic pot, let the medium soak, and drain it.

A quick tip on bringing home a brand new orchid flower: it is advisable to place your orchid somewhere away from your other home plants (if you have any). This is a sort of a short quarantine to give yourself some time to observe the Phalaenopsis and check for any signs of pests, mold, or diseases (such as tiny critters on the leaves and the root system, wet black spots on the leaves which tend to expand, foul smell of the soil when it's moist, etc.) . This way you minimize the risk of transferring these malevolent agents to the other plants!

Where do I put my own Phalaenopsis?

I live in a small South facing apartment in a country with a combination of temperate-continental climate, but in recent years it has been slowly moving towards the Mediterranean climate type. So, in general, there is lots of light coming in during most of the year. That is why I have put my orchids on the window sill behind the balcony (to reduce the number of hours with direct sunlight). In the summer I roll the blinds down (I use a specific type of fabric blinds called "day and night" for better control of the amount of light) to protect the plant from burning. And that's it!

Dry yellow leaf from exposure to direct sunlight ↓↓↓

sign of a direct light burn

@Milky Green

Room temperature and humidity

When it comes to choosing the best placement of your plant, you need to take into consideration another vital parameter – the temperature of the room.

There is a very easy rule to determine this – if you feel comfortable, your orchid will most likely be comfortable as well. The best temperature range is between 60° F and 86° F (16° C to 30° C). Try not to place your Phalaenopsis in a spot outside this range for long periods of time – the extremely low temperatures will slow (or completely stop) its growth and promote root and leaf rotting; while high temperatures will dehydrate and burn the plant.

As far as the humidity of the room goes, the Phalaenopsis orchid does well within the range of 40% to 70%. As I mentioned in the tools section of this book (at the end of this volume), it is best to have some sort of thermometer and a hygrometer to make sure you have covered the basic needs of your plants for temperature and humidity. If the air in your living space is too dry (because of the climate or as a result of air conditioning), consider getting an air humidifier. Well, it is not just good for the orchids – your own lungs and the mucosa of your respiratory system will be extremely happy as well! I personally use an aroma diffuser which works as a humidifier as well. It has been a very useful tool during the hot summer days and in the winter when we typically use an air conditioner.

Again, the best way to check whether you have made the right decisions is to inspect your orchid frequently and monitor its behavior. There are a couple of easy signs you can decode and make some tweaks, if necessary.

Here's what I am looking for when inspecting my plant:

1. ***The color of the leaves*** – if the leaves rapidly start getting yellow and dry, the most likely reason is intense direct sunlight and high temperatures; Try changing the spot, rolling down the blinds and hydrating on a tight schedule (more about that in the section on watering). Also note that it is normal for the orchid to naturally lose 1-2 leaves per year from the base of the plant. However, if the Phal's leaves are quickly getting wrinkly, yellow, and dry, it is most likely due to excessive direct sunlight.

2. ***The texture of the leaves*** – the leaves of a healthy orchid must be large and thick. If you notice them becoming wrinkly and soft, consider watering the plant a bit more often (again, take a look at the chapter on watering). Also, make sure you check the humidity of the space and consider misting the plants often or investing in a humidifier;

3. ***The size of the new leaves*** – each newly formed leaf should naturally be larger (or

pretty much the same size as the previous one beneath it). Well, this is not an infinite process, but if you notice that the newly formed leaves are getting smaller and smaller, that's a sign that the plant is experiencing stress. It is not growing well, and it might need better nourishment – (take a look at the chapters on root inspection, watering and fertilizing).

Note: the smaller leaves situation is more concerning when it comes to old plants that you have owned for some time.

Conversely, a brand new orchid may initially produce smaller leaves. This is often due to the environmental shock it is experiencing. The plant had been under optimal conditions in the nursery, then it was transported into the place it was sold, and finally – it arrived at our home. So, in this whole ordeal, the orchid may be a bit stressed and its first couple of leaves it develops may be much smaller than usual. Also, another possible outcome from acquiring a brand new plant is the old roots dying off. This is nothing to be too worried about, too. The old root system had been accustomed to certain growing conditions which may be quite different from what you would offer. The important thing to look for in these situations is whether these issues tend to persist for long periods of time. The general rule of thumb is a healthy Phalaenopsis orchid developing about 2-3 new leaves per year which are the same size or bigger.

So, in conclusion, if your orchid looks fine and is growing well, chances are you have put it in the right spot at the right temperature.

Can you place your orchid outside?

So far I have covered the correct placement of your Phal indoors. But if you are wondering if you can put your plant somewhere outside closed doors, here's my take on this subject.

There is nothing wrong with keeping your orchids outside as long as the necessary conditions are met – no direct sunlight, appropriate temperatures and humidity, no strong cold or hot air drafts, etc. In some cases this may even be a better option since we can supply better ventilation for the foliage and the root system. And orchids love some good ventilation for their epiphytic nature. Sometimes the air inside our living spaces can become a bit stale, and this is something you should definitely take care of.

However, my biggest problem with the outside placement is the higher risk of pest infestations. A plant in the balcony or in the garden may serve as the perfect hub for the growth, nourishment, and reproduction of all kinds of insects and critters. Just take a look at the photo below which was sent to me by a dear friend!

@Milky Green

Her Phalaenopsis orchid and its petals have become a sort of a nursery for a pregnant stink bug. Yikes! And this happened because the plant was placed near an open window without a fly net installed!

That is why I think it is best for complete beginners, who are inexperienced with pest control, to keep their Phals indoors, at least at the beginning. I personally supply the necessary ventilation by keeping my plants near open windows in the summer. However, they all have fly nets installed, so that there are no insects flying inside the house. In the winter I ventilate the living space with fresh air by opening the windows for an hour daily (or half an hour twice a day). I also make sure there are no strong air drafts while I do this procedure. In such cases I need to remove the orchids away from the air currant beforehand.

Now let's move to the major topic you are probably eager to learn about – how, how often, and how much to water your orchid!

HOW AND WHEN TO
WATER YOUR ORCHID

*T*his is probably the most controversial and most misunderstood topic about growing a Phalaenopsis (and any other orchid as well).

When I was looking for this information online and offline, I kept getting the same answer – *"Do not water your plant too much!"*

But what does that mean? How much is too much? So, basically, for the longest time I had been growing my orchid as a cactus. :-D And logically, it wasn't doing well! The leaves were getting smaller, limpy, and wrinkly. Not to mention that the plant hadn't blossomed in years! Actually, it NEVER blossomed again after its purchase.

So, here's your first sign of dehydration – soft and wrinkly leaves. If your orchid has those, read this chapter carefully.

OK, now what? How often do you water your Phalaenopsis? Is it once a week, every two weeks, every 3 days?

The bad news is there is no one size fits all type of answer. The period between each watering should be individual depending on the room temperature, the amount of sunlight, the humidity (or dryness) of the air, the season, the type and the amount of medium, the size of the pot, etc.

The good news is there are simple signs you can check to determine when to hydrate your plant. Let's take a look!

1. *The color of the roots* – we are looking at the color of the roots **inside** the pot. That is why it is best to use a transparent pot to check how the roots are doing (at least in the beginning). Plus, it helps with the photosynthesis. Yes, that's the quirky thing about orchids – they photosynthesize with their root system as a back-up plan in case the leaves are damaged. So, dry roots have a light green-grayish color. Just take a quick look at the airy ones outside the pot – they are usually dry and you can compare them to the ones inside the pot. If you are unsure, just wait a day or two to avoid overwatering.

2. *Condensation* – sometimes the visible roots at the walls of the pot look dry but the ones hidden on the inside may still be moist. So, to avoid root rot, we have to be sure all roots are almost dry and ready for watering. The telltale sign is the little droplets of H_2O on the walls of the pot. If the plant is placed in a warm room, the extra water will condensate and it will be visible (usually in the morning or at noon). If there is any condensation visible, wait for a

couple more days until it disappears before hydrating the plant!

Here's a quick tip: if these droplets remain for too long, this may be a sign that the roots are not ventilated well. In this case, to avoid root rot, drill (or slice) some holes into the pot to let more air in. Be careful not to damage the roots and use all your gardening tools with all safety measures necessary!

Here's how dry roots look like in the flower pot:

@Milky Green

Here's how dry airy roots look like outside the flower pot:

Here's a small example why I think that there is no one-size-fits-all type of watering schedule. Below you can see two pots side by side. These are filled with the exact same potting medium and they are placed in the exact same environment. I watered the plants on the exact same time, and in four days this is what we can see. The pot on the left is already dry and ready for its next watering, while the pot on the right is still moist and can wait for a few more days. This is because the size of the pot on the left is smaller and can fit less potting medium (and thus retain less water). Moreover, I couldn't fill the small pot as tight as the bigger one, and the large air pockets contribute to the faster water evaporation. So, as you can see, this is a very simple example why each plant should have its own watering schedule. Also, this is the main reason why I like labeling my plants and creating reminders on my phone to keep track of each flower individually. If this seems like an overkill, do not worry – in time and with practice you will get the handle of the process and you will build a habit of monitoring your Phals regularly.

How to water your plant?

The watering procedure for orchids is a bit different than the one for regular house plants.
Now is the perfect time to explain some of the specifics of the Orchidaceae family.
First, again we need to take a look at the natural habitat of orchids – these beautiful plants grow on trees partially covered in moss instead of regular soil. Their roots are floating in the air which means that they are being constantly ventilated and drained from excess water.
This information is necessary to understand why orchids should be watered in a different manner and why over-hydration can be detrimental to their health and wellbeing.

Let's begin!

You will need a container larger than the plant's pot.
Place the orchid inside and gently pour water into the container until it submerges the whole pot.
The quality of the water is also important and here's why. Remember that the Phalaenopsis's roots are no normal roots. Actually, the real roots are very thin and gentle (like a thin thread) enveloped by the green fleshy part we see (called velamen). This

additional layer of coating is the plant's back-up plan for photosynthesis. In other words, the root system should be as clean as possible (the part which is exposed to sunlight) and we should not let any deposits to form – limescale, Chlorine, rust from old pipes, dirt, excessive amounts of chemicals from fertilization, etc.

That is why it is best to use as clean water as possible – distilled water or filtered. I personally use a charcoal filter pitcher and my orchids love the soft and tasty H2O from it! As a last resort, you can use tap water but let it sit for a couple of hours to let all the impurities sink down the container.

Now that the orchid is fully covered with water, let the soil soak for about 15 minutes and then, fully drain.

In the meantime, you can show some love to the airy roots by spraying them with some clean water as well!

Note: do not mist the blooms! *If your orchid is currently in bloom, it is best to avoid spraying the flowers with water. In some cases, the combination between low temperatures (during which the Phalaenopsis plant typically produces blooms) and humidity creates the perfect environment for mold and fungus to develop. So, regular misting of the flowers may cause them to become infected and get* *some unpleasant black spots which are impossible to remove.*

Finally, one important action you may need to take! Naturally, orchids are tilted towards the ground and the rain water is freely flowing down the plant and into the ground. At home, that's not always the case. Most store-bought orchids are erected and there is a risk of excess water remaining inside the core of the plant and causing rotting (especially if the temperatures are low and the area is humid). I personally have never had this issue, but in case you wish to be strict, absorb the moisture with a paper tissue just to be safe!

Also, gently wipe the leaves and remove any dust or dirt off to improve their ability to absorb light and to photosynthesize!

Important note! Do not wipe the back of the leaves! *At the underside of the orchid leaves are located special types of structures called stomata. The stomata consists of small pores invisible to the naked eye which take an important part in the "breathing" process of the plant – the entry of carbon dioxide for photosynthesis purposes, as well as evaporating water (transpiration). By aggressively wiping the back of the leaves, these pores may become* *damaged and clogged, thus hindering these vital processes!*

And that's it! Return the plant to its spot and wait for the signs of dehydration, and repeat the watering procedure.

I personally set a reminder on my phone so I do not forget to check on my orchid and to remember when the last time I watered it was. In my case, I usually water my Phalaenopsis roughly once every week throughout the year, and every 4-5 days during the summer.

But, again, you do you! Your schedule may be different according to your region and the micro climate of your home!

Note: if you are a fan of water conservation, you can use the liquid left from the hydration process to water your other unpretentious plants. I have tested this with my Amaryllis, Rain Lily, Jade plant, and an Aechmea (Bromeliad) – they all have been growing very well ever since!

But you do you! If you are anxious about re-using the water from the orchid, just throw it away in the toilet or the sink.

An important side note: *do not share the water of a brand new orchid (or an orchid you suspect is* *infected with a disease or pests) with other plants. These ailments may get transferred to the other flowers.*

HOW AND WHEN TO FERTILIZE YOUR ORCHID

*T*his is probably the next big topic right after the watering process and for a reason – this is basically the food that the plants need to grow properly and to produce their magnificent blooms year after year! There are many options to pick from and everyone has their preferred way of nurturing their Phalaenopsis plants. But here's what I would suggest based on how I grow my own moon orchids and how I get the desired results. I know there are plenty of universal fertilizers (usually with a 20-20-20 ratio which is 20% nitrogen, 20% phosphorus, 20% potassium) out there which can be used all year round. However, I think that implementing two separate products is the best way to go about it. Because there are two distinct growth periods each year which any Phalaenopsis goes through. This means that there have to be specific nutrients to assist the plant in each one of them.

→ *Fertilizers for growth* – the most popular varieties are liquid growth fertilizers for the main root system and spray ones for the airy roots during the growth period. This is usually a high-nitrogen type of plant food with the 30-10-10 ratio which consists of 30% nitrogen, 10% phosphorus, and 10% potassium. The Phalaenopsis orchids have one long period of growth which usually happens between March and September in the Northern hemisphere (when the temperatures are high). This is their time of growing new leaves and roots (both inside the pot and airy roots as well). So, the proper nutrients have to accommodate the plant's need for better and faster growth in order for it to gather strength for the blooming season (which definitely requires lots of energy which the orchid has to muster beforehand). I believe that if the Phalaenopsis flower hadn't been treated well with suitable fertilizing and watering during its growth season, the blooming process would be almost impossible.

→ *Fertilizers for blooming* – again, they usually come as liquid growth fertilizers for the main root system and spray ones for the airy roots during the blooming period. This is usually a high-phosphorus type of plant food with the 10-30-20 ratio which consists of 10% nitrogen, 30% phosphorus, and 20% potassium. The blooming season (usually happens when there is a significant difference between day and nighttime temperatures) is very important for the orchid plants in securing their pollination process and the continuation of their species. And this process requires lots of energy and nutrients to achieve this aim. Let's not forget that the Phalaenopsis orchid has some of the most long-lasting blossoms and this takes effort on the plant's end. So, there are special fertilizing products which are specifically designed to help the moon orchids produce more flowers which would last longer, and which would provide the best compounds and substances the plant needs in this endeavor. So, I highly recommend you grab some orchid food for blooming and commence using it when the nighttime temperatures start to drop and the first flower stalks would start to appear!

Please note that one common mistake, in my own opinion, when growing this plant family is trying to force it to produce flowers by intensive fertilization for blooming (the second type of orchid food). This is not always possible because the plant needs a solid base and stamina to bloom.

This is our main goal throughout the year – to boost the orchid, to take good care of it in the growing process, to keep it properly hydrated and fed, so when the blooming season comes, it is ready to produce flowers.

The fertilization process is also very easy, but the tricky part is to dose it properly. Over fertilization is detrimental to the plant and it could lead to "burning" the root system.

So, here's my method!
I use liquid plant food specifically designed for orchids.
Read the instructions of the plant food you have chosen carefully, and check the recommended frequency for fertilizing.
For example, the brand I am using suggests feeding the plant once every week between March and October, and once every two weeks between November and February (in the Northern hemisphere).
But I am always trying to be extra cautious, so I decided to take a much more conservative strategy when it comes to fertilization. I feel this schedule may be too intensive which could lead to chemical deposits on the roots.
So, my personal approach is to feed my orchid once a month. So far this strategy has been very successful – my plants have been growing fast and healthy, they started to reproduce and create extra orchids

(called keikis which can be propagated), and each plant produces flower stalks packed with beautiful long-lasting blooms year after year!

Plus, the root system looks perfectly healthy and "happy" during my regular root inspections.

Note: over fertilization, root burns, or excessive chemical deposits (white spots on the medium which usually mean accumulated salts from hard water or excessive fertilizing) usually cause the roots to become dark, almost black. So, if you decide to go with a more ambitious feeding schedule, check frequently for these signs, and tweak your feeding strategy accordingly. Also, it is best to perform "a flush" at least once a month. This procedure is like regular watering using distilled, reverse osmosis or filtered water. The goal is to dissolve any accumulated chemicals and deposits as much as possible.

The fertilization process

Now that you have picked your preferred plant food, take out the container you usually use for watering the orchid.

Dissolve the fertilizer (follow the directions of the product for the proper dosage; in my case, the dosage is one bottle cap) in clean filtered water.

Dip the plant in the container until the pot is fully submerged – just like you would do in the watering procedure.

Actually, this is just like regular hydration with added fertilizer. Remember that this counts as watering – check for the same signs of dehydration before fertilizing the plant.

Again, in about 15-20 minutes take out the orchid, drain the excess water and remove any moisture from the crown of the plant (the base of the leaves).

And that's it!

If you need to, set reminders on your phone, so you don't forget when the last fertilization or watering was. Keep monitoring your plant for signs of dehydration, over hydration, over fertilization, etc.

Just a reminder:

Soft, limp, leathery, and wrinkly leaves = dehydration;

Dark roots = over fertilization;

Dark brown, mushy roots, and foul smell of the moist medium = over watering, not enough ventilation, and root rot.

What to do with the dissolved fertilizer?

You can throw it away in the toilet or the sink, but I am not a fan of wasting water.

I personally use it to water and fertilize my other plants to conserve water. So far I haven't had any negative side effects. On the contrary, my ornamental bulbous plants have been blooming and growing steadily ever since.

For example, I have one type of Amaryllis and a Rain Lily – they both have been feeling quite well with the orchid fertilizer (both the one for growth and the one for blooming)!

HOW AND WHEN TO RE-POT YOUR ORCHID

*L*et's say you have your brand-new orchid (which is usually sold while it is blooming), you have put it in the right spot, you have been watering it and fertilizing it correctly, and now the blooming period is over.

What to do next?

After the blooming period of a newly bought orchid is over, I would highly suggest you repot your plant with fresh soil and perform a thorough root inspection.

We will talk a lot about the blooming and re-blooming process a bit later in the book. But for now, for the purpose of taking the next steps in the right direction, I will simply note that after all the flowers wither and fall off, it is best to cut off the stalk at its base without harming the leaves. This is usually at about 1 cm height or half an inch.

Do not worry – the plant will create a new one for the next season! By cutting it off it will immediately direct all the resources the stalk drains (water and minerals) into the next phase of the Phalaenopsis' life – growth!

There are a few more situations when it is advisable to repot your Phalaenopsis. Here are the most common ones:

➔ *Every two years for prevention purposes* – the organic medium (bark chips, moss, coconut husk, etc.) decomposes in time, and it increases the acidity inside the pot. And this can hurt the plant and its ability to absorb nutrients long term. Old dead roots also tend to change the pH of the soil, and it is best to be removed periodically. On the other hand, repotting your Phalaenopsis too often will cause stress and slow down its growth and the production of flowers. So, every two years is a good rule of thumb, if there are no other serious issues with the orchid – see the next points.

➔ *Root rot* – this is something tightly related to the previous point but it is a much more serious situation which needs to be addresses ASAP. If you notice that the medium smells bad when it's moist, this is probably due to some tissues rotting, and you should schedule a repotting immediately. Also, if you water and fertilize your Phal regularly, but it keeps looking dehydrated and malnourished, there may be a serious problem with the roots. So, a root inspection is highly recommended at this point.

Pests – if you notice any critters moving around the soil, move the orchid away from the rest of your flowers, and start repotting and treating the infestation ASAP. Feel free to get the *"Orchid Pests and Diseases - Diagnosis, Treatment and Prevention"* book by Sue Bottom. It will give you some great practical knowledge of the most common orchid ailments and pests, as well as how to treat them successfully.

Here's what I would suggest you do!

First, carefully cut off the flower stalk with a sharp tool.

Next, soak the plant in clean water for about 15-20 minutes and drain – just like you would do in a regular watering procedure.

Third, take a large container (for example a plastic washing basin or a tray) and transfer the plant along with the soil inside. Remember to wear protective gloves! (*The gloves not only protect your own skin, but also all of your other plants. Let's say that one of your orchids is plagued by pests or mold. Using bare hands may cause you to easily transfer these malevolent agents into all the other plants you have at your home. So, if you are repotting a brand new flower or one that has some sort of health issues, make sure you use a fresh pair of gloves and change*

them or disinfect them thoroughly when you move to handing   a   different   plant!)
Now, remove the soil and gently dislodge all bark chips which may had stuck to the roots. Start inspecting each and every root. We are looking for dark brown-black mushy roots which are affected by root rot. Also, we can remove all fully dried out and withered roots which are completely dead. Be conservative with the root system removal process. For example, you can see some roots are pale yellow but with firm texture – they are completely healthy. They simply hadn't been exposed to sunlight and hadn't synthesized enough chlorophyll.

Completely dry root:

@Milky Green

Also, you may see some roots which look thin and mushy in the middle, but healthy green at the end – they are also healthy and can be preserved. The reason for this lies in the specific structure of the root system. As you may remember, the real root of the orchid looks like a thin thread enveloped in a thick coating (called velamen), designed to help the plant with the process of photosynthesis.

Sometimes, this coating can be damaged but the root inside remains intact, healthy, and perfectly functioning. So, I would advise you to keep these as well! The more roots we have and the stronger they are, the healthier the plant will be and the more blooms we will enjoy in the future!

So, carefully remove the dead roots both inside the pot and outside (the airy ones which are dry or rotten) with a sharp sterilized gardening tool (please, follow all safety measures when operating with these sharp objects!). Just to recap – we are looking for roots which are soft, mushy, and papery-hollow to the touch. These are the ones that need to be cut off. The logic behind it is that this dead or damaged velamen will continue to decompose and change the acidity of the medium. In time, this may harm the healthy roots, and cause them to become unviable for absorbing nutrients.

Now, here comes a very important and often missing part – we need to disinfect the root system. This will prevent any malevolent microorganisms, pathogens, fungi, and rotting processes from destroying the healthy roots!

For this purpose I use a simple solution of hydrogen peroxide 6% diluted in the same amount of clean or distilled water (or simply use the 3% option). I know some people do not dilute the peroxide, but I am always trying to be extra cautious and avoid burning the plant.

Mix both ingredients in a spray bottle (please, remember to put a label on the bottle and to store it in a safe place away from children and pets!), shake well, and lavishly cover the roots with the solution.

Wait for several minutes for the peroxide to do its magic (you will notice a slight fizzing sound or frothing).

Note: hydrogen peroxide is very unstable. In contact with air it quickly decomposes to oxygen and water. This means that it is best use freshly opened bottle to get the maximum benefit of the substance. The peroxide is considered to be best for 3 months after opening the bottle. But if you use the liquid from an opened bottle, and you don't hear any fizzing sounds, it is best to use fresh one from a sealed container.

A quick leaf inspection

During this re-potting process it is best to use this opportunity to perform a quick leaf inspection as well.

Take a close look at the base of the leaves to check for dark sports and decay. If so, this might be a sign of leaf rot. Do not underestimate this issue since it might lead to complete loss of leaves, inability to photosynthesize, stagnation, inability to re-bloom, and even the death of the plant.

To correct this, use the same disinfecting solution and leave it to work for several minutes. Then, remove the extra moisture with a paper tissue. Repeat this often and most importantly – keep the base of the flower dry after each watering. Also, consider increasing the room temperature and improving the ventilation of the room.

As far as removing leaves, I would advise you to avoid this as much as possible. Cut off only the ones which are completely dry and withered. Yellow, soft, and wrinkled leaves are a sign of dehydration or over exposure to direct sunlight, but they are still viable and perfectly functioning and photosynthesizing parts of the plant. Remember that the orchid needs all the strength it can gather to continuously grow and bloom over and over again!

Then, finally, we can re-pot the orchid in fresh soil. Remember to use potting soil specifically designed for orchids. It usually contains bark chips and a little bit of moss. There are also medium types which are fortified with slow release fertilizers, so take this into account when creating your feeding schedule! I am currently using such type of soil, and as I have already mentioned, I fertilize my Phalaenopsis only once a month!

I would also recommend you avoid the soil blends which contain a lot of moss since it absorbs lots of water and it could potentially lead to root rot. This rule would be mostly suitable if you live in an area with a moderate climate and the temperatures may drop often. If you feel that your potting mix contains too much moss, it retains too much moisture for a long time, and the risks of mold formation are high, consider getting some extra bark chips. Add them to the medium and they will improve the drainage of the plant.

On the flip side, if you live in a hot and dry area, and your plant dehydrates fast and easily, grab some sphagnum moss, and add it to the mix. Remember to place some of the moss on top of the pot around the airy roots. This will seal the moisture inside the planter and prevent the water from quickly evaporating. It may take some experimenting until you find the right consistency and the correct ratio of each component of the potting soil. Keep monitoring the growth of your plant to see how it reacts to the changes.

As far as the pot goes, I would recommend getting the most common transparent orchid pots which give the plant extra sunlight and a better chance to photosynthesize!

Also, if you have noticed lots of root rot and if you are worried it might re-occur, you can choose a container with extra holes (or slashes) on the walls. Or you can also drill your own holes or make a couple of incisions with a utility knife (please, be careful and stay safe when using sharp tools, and keep them away from children!). This will give the root system some extra aeration!

Remember to take into account the size of the orchid and its root system as well. If the Phalaenopsis is small with very few healthy roots left, take a smaller pot. Otherwise, the plant may "feel" the need to occupy the free space with lots of new roots. This is not necessarily a bad thing, but it could cause the orchid to skip one blooming season.

Remember that this plant family is extremely sturdy and probably one of the few that feels comfortable in small pots.

Here's an example from my personal experience just to give you a clearer picture. My first Phalaenopsis have grown into three joined plants, and it was continuously blooming (creating more than one flower spikes) in its original pot (5 inch in diameter). Of course, after reaching such size and after the roots had been growing rapidly out of the pot, I re-potted it in a larger container (with a 7.5 inch diameter). Another option in such scenario is to divide it into three different plants and place them in three individual small pots (more about this in the chapter on propagation).

The potting process is fairly easy. Put some of the soil at the bottom of the container. Start placing the plant inside as you continue to put more soil in-between the roots. Remember not to jam-pack the pot. Leave some breathing and growing space for the roots to avoid rotting (a crucial requirement for all epiphytes which do not grow in regular soil). Conversely, try not to leave any large air pockets as well. These are nothing to worry about, but keep in mind that the medium may dry out faster. So, make sure you keep an eye on your plant, and follow the guidelines I described in the chapter on watering to create the ideal hydration schedule. Cover the plant with more bark chips and that's it!

Do not try to fit all the roots inside. There will always be some which will remain in the air and that's totally fine! Here's an interesting info bit about airy roots — they are much more adapted to absorbing moisture from the atmosphere, rather than the soil. So, they are better off outside the pot anyway. Just remember to hydrate them during the watering process with some clean aqua and a spray bottle.

Finally, soak the plant in clean water once again, drain it completely, and place it at your favorite preferred spot!

At this point, you can create your watering and fertilizing schedule accordingly (with a specific type of fertilizer for growth instead of one for blooming!).

You can also mark down the date of the re-potting and schedule the next one in about two years' time (in case the plant is growing well and does not need another root inspection much sooner).

HELP YOUR ORCHID BLOOM CONTINOUSLY

*T*his is probably the most interesting part of growing an orchid. After all, this is the main reason we get such a plant – it produces delicate, beautiful and long-lasting flowers.

But a lot of people get frustrated when their Phalaenopsis just won't re-bloom again and again after its purchase.

So, in this chapter I will show you my philosophy and proven strategy for stimulating this plant to keep producing flowers over and over again.

First, note that I used the word "stimulate" rather than "force". I keep seeing various tutorials where people claim that you can force your plant to bloom using extreme measures, like placing ice cubes in the soil.

I personally don't think that's reasonable and this could lead to serious damages to the plant in the long run (I am not even sure if it really works). If we take care of our plant well, nourish it throughout the whole growing season (spring and summer), it will have the strength to produce flower spikes and bloom continuously.

So, the first and most vital step in the blooming process is to have a healthy well-nourished plant.

This incorporates all the activities I mentioned previously:

> *Having an appropriate watering schedule;*
> *Having a suitable well-balanced fertilizing plan with specific plant food for growth;*
> *Having a healthy well-maintained and well-developed root system free from rot and pests;*
> *Having large, strong and well-developed leaves able to photosynthesize – as many as possible.*

Having all these conditions in place and with a little boost, we can expect our orchid to have the necessary life force to produce more and more flower spikes, more and more (and larger) blooms every year without fail.

Now what's that boost I am talking about?

Naturally, when growing orchids in a climate with four seasons, the growing period is usually during spring and summer. Once the temperatures start to drop (during fall and winter), we can expect the first flower stalks to show up.

The trick to help the plant produce them is to emulate the blooming conditions in its natural habitat – namely to create the necessary temperature difference compared to the one we have in the summer.

This means that during the day, the orchid should be exposed to normal temperatures which are perfectly comfortable to us humans – around 23-27° C (74-80° F). Whereas during the night, these can drop to the necessary minimum without freezing the plant – 16-17° C (60-62° F).

Here's what I do – I place the Phalaenopsis in a well-lit spot (during the winter this does not burn the leaves) which is air-conditioned to the necessary temperature (usually 25° C/77° F). At night, I switch off the heating or leave it to maintain the minimum of 16° C/60° F (in case the winter is very cold and there's a risk of over-cooling the room).

As you can see, this is pretty much the only boost you can apply to make your plant start blooming. In areas where the night temperatures start dropping early, the orchids may commence producing flowers in October (in the Northern hemisphere). In my case, since my apartment is facing south and it is well-insulated, my orchids start blooming in late December until May.

A problem may arise in areas where the climate is steady and continuously hot and dry. In this case, you have to artificially create the necessary conditions. For example, keep your flower in a mildly warm room away from direct sunlight, and switch on your preferred cooling system at night at the proper temperature (16-17° C /60-62° F). This has to stimulate your plant to produce blooms! Just make sure it is not exposed to strong direct cold air drafts.

Now, once you see there is a flower spike coming up, you have to change the feeding schedule a little bit.

You can recognize it by two main signs:

1. The flower stalk usually grows between the last and the penultimate leaf. In comparison, the roots are usually growing directly after the bottom most leaf.
   Note: in rare cases the orchid may produce a flower spike which comes directly from the heart of the crown (the very top of the plant where the latest leaf had emerged). This is called a terminal spike and it is very likely that the orchid is not going to continue growing and producing more leaves in the future. In other words, it is very likely that the plant is going to perish in the near future (in about 1-2 years' time).

2. The color of the flower spike is greener, shinier, and it starts to form a peculiar shape with tiny buds – most orchid lovers describe

them as mitten-shaped. Whereas, the typical root likewise has a shiny green top, but it quickly turns into its natural pale-greyish color.

As the flower spike keeps growing, you will realize that it is not just another root coming out, even if you are a complete beginner.

As soon as you confirm that the plant is blooming, you can immediately switch the fertilizer with the type suitable for producing more, larger, and long-lasting flowers.

Again, I am taking the safe road, and I fertilize my plant once a month instead of the recommended frequency of once a week or once every two weeks. This strategy has been working very well and the root system looks good and healthy, which is my most important indicator for the fertilizing intensity.

If your roots are getting darker and darker, consider feeding the plant less often and watering with neutral clean water free from chlorine and limescale (distilled or filtered).

The feeding and watering procedures remain the same! The only thing you need to keep in mind is the appropriate temperature difference and fertilization for blooming. That's it!

Remember to purchase some sort of a support stick and some clips to keep the flower spike upward and prevent it from breaking or bending forward (which would increase the risk of toppling the pot over)!

Bud blast

A bud blast is when the blooms of the Phalaenopsis (or any other type of orchid) start to dry off and fall down prematurely before they open (or before they open fully). This phenomenon is quite frustrating and disheartening because the main reason why we acquire these magnificent plants is for their beautiful flowers. Right?

So, in this section I will do my best to explain why this may happen sometimes and how to prevent it as much as possible. And I focus on prevention because I think (and in my experience), once this process starts, it may be irreversible. Well, at least for that particular blooming season.

Now, why do buds blast?

The short answer is stress. My observations and my logic behind it is that for whatever reason the survival instinct of the plant kicked in, and it started withdrawing its energy from the blooming process and directing it into withstanding the stress or the shock it is currently experiencing. So, let's see what the common sources of stress might be!

➜ *Environmental shock*

I think this is the biggest cause of buds blasting, at least in my experience. I have seen this phenomenon happen mainly to newly purchased orchids. That is why I think that the sudden changes of their environment cause them to sacrifice the blooms in effort to survive and withstand the shock. Most orchids come from large-scale farms where they had been living in optimal conditions, so that they grow and produce flowers as fast as possible. But as soon as this happens, they are quickly transported to all sorts of retailers and shops, sometimes even to foreign countries around the world. So, all these rapid changes and even long-term neglect along the way, may contribute to the Phalaenopsis not being able to fully bloom and sustain these blooms for a long time. In that case, all you need to do is try to offer your plant the best possible conditions you are able to – the necessary temperature, water, food, ventilation, light, and humidity. This way it will gather enough strength for the next blooming seasons ahead! Also, try not to make sudden radical changes to your orchid regarding these parameters. Phalaenopsis's are sturdy and adaptable, but they have their limits. Here are a few examples:

- *neglecting the watering and fertilizing schedule and the orchid becoming dehydrated and depleted of nutrients mid-blooming;*
- *being exposed to extremely low or hot temperatures;*
- *being exposed to strong cold or hot air drafts* (try to keep the plant at a safe distance from air conditioners and heaters), etc.

➜ *Diseases and pests*

Every disease puts the plant into extreme stress and it is only natural for its survival instincts to switch on. I have mentioned the most common ones are root and crown rot. In this case, prevention is key. This includes:

- ✓ *avoiding leaving water in the crown (especially in winter);*
- ✓ *avoiding over-watering;*
- ✓ *changing the medium about every two years;*
- ✓ *changing the medium when there is root rot (notice if there are any foul smells when the medium is moist);*
- ✓ *removing any dead roots and disinfecting the root system;*

If there's any rotting process happening during the blooming season and the buds start to blast, it is best to repot the plant ASAP, remove any dead rotting tissues, and disinfecting with hydrogen peroxide 3%. If you notice any crown rot, try to do this procedure immediately – this situation could be detrimental to the plant, and it could kill it in a matter of days.

Another main cause of the buds blasting which goes into this category is *Botrytis cinerea*. This is a type of fungus which affects mostly plants and fruits, including the Phalaenopsis orchid and its blooms. The main source of this ailment is again the detrimental combination of moisture, lack of proper ventilation, and low temperatures (very rarely it may happen at higher temperatures) – this is the perfect habitat of all sorts of bacteria and fungi to grow. So, once again – it is best to avoid leaving any liquids remaining on the plant, especially on the blossoms – they are much more fragile than the leaves and roots. That is why in the chapter on hydration I suggested you don't mist your blooms during the watering and fertilizing processes. The mild cases may look like small dark spots on the petals, but in severe cases, this might lead to the complete destruction of the blossoms and bud blasts.

The same goes with any pest infestations. But since this topic is rather big and intricate, and I don't have any available footage, I would like to direct you to one excellent booklet called *"Orchid Pests and Diseases - Diagnosis, Treatment and Prevention"* by Sue Bottom. There you will find the most common ailments on orchids, including the Phalaenopsis type.

➜ *Exposure to gas, especially ethylene*

Most orchids are very sensitive to many types of gases, and it is best to keep them away from any appliances which may have some emissions in the air. This also includes the ethylene gas which is emitted from fruits. Yes, that's right! Keep your Phals away from fruits of any sort, especially those who are fully ripe and on the verge of rotting!

Help! My orchid isn't blooming!

In this section I will do my best to list some of the most common reasons why your Phalaenopsis orchid is not blooming. Because that's one of the most frustrating and discouraging situations for any beginner orchid grower. I hope I can give you some easy and practical solutions and telltale signs to look for to determine what the main cause is, and how to address this issue.

➜ *The plant's biological clock is out of sync*

This usually happens to brand-new orchids which were induced to bloom off-season. As I mentioned previously, the Phalaenopsis orchids have two main seasons throughout the year – one for growth and one for producing blooms. But most large-scale orchid farms have a continuous cycle of producing blooming plants all year round by artificially creating the perfect blooming conditions once the orchid is mature enough to produce flowers. This is why we have blooming Phals in the summer. But what happens when you bring that plant into your home? The flower would need quite some time to adjust to its new environment and sync its natural biological clock to the current season. And more often than not, the Phal will skip the next blooming season, especially if it had already been induced to bloom in a greenhouse in the summer. This might be something a bit similar to us humans experiencing a jet lag. In this situation you don't really have to worry too much. Just provide the best conditions as you can, monitor if the plant is growing well, and it will muster the energy to bloom the following autumn/winter.

➜ *The orchid is not adjusted to its new environment*

This is something tightly related to the first point. The Phalaenopsis plants are adjustable to the conditions they live in (within their limits). And they might experience quite a shock if these parameters change rapidly – the amount of light, water, nutrients, humidity, ventilation, etc. Again, this issue might be more related to newly purchased plants or when there are some significant changes in your home environment. If the orchid becomes too stressed, it may very well skip one blooming season in an effort to adjust to the change. Give it time to adjust and continue providing the necessary growing conditions. If you need to, go back to the section on bud blast where I mentioned the signs and main causes of stress for the Phalaenopsis orchid.

➜ *The orchid does not have enough strength*

This is also something quite similar to the previous two points. But it is much more common to old plants that you have been having around for quite some time, and they are just not willing to bloom. In my opinion, the main cause for this is any form of setback. A setback can be anything which causes the plant to be put to a challenge – improper environmental conditions, a disease, pest infestations etc. The more sever the case, the more time the plant would need to recover and get back on track with growth and blooming. So, look for any kinds of anomalies and signs of a problem. Is the orchid dehydrated? Has it been severely dehydrated for a long time? Are there any signs of a disease or pests? Is the crown rotting and are the leaves progressively getting yellow and falling off excessively (especially from the crown)? Has your orchid been recovering from such conditions recently? Are there any signs of root rot – black mushy roots and bad smells when the medium is moist? Do your best to make an assessment if the plant is growing well or if there is something really wrong that needs to be addressed ASAP.

→ *Improper conditions for blooming*

As I noted previously, the perfect conditions for an orchid to bloom is that optimal temperature difference. This is one of the most important factors that will induce your orchid to bloom. The temperature drop in the autumn and winter tells the plant that the blooming season has commenced and it needs to start developing its flower spike. Out of curiosity, one winter I decided to leave the air conditioner on to maintain a steady 25° C (77° F), and the result was not that shocking – my orchids didn't bloom. They just continued their vegetative mode and kept creating new leaves and roots. So, the temperature fluctuation is a must!

➔ *The plant is not mature enough*

This applies mainly to newly purchased orchid seedlings or small keikis (baby orchids). The typical Phalaenopsis plant needs at least three years of growth under optimal conditions to be old enough to produce flowers. So, if you are in this situation, no worries – just arm yourself with patience! This does not apply to orchids which had produced flower spikes at least once in the past. So, if you got your plant without any blooms, look for old cut off spikes to check if it had bloomed previously.

This is how an old dried out spike looks like:

old cut off spike

@Milky Green

Re-blooming from the same flower spike (sequential blooming)

In the first edition of this book I mentioned that most Phalaenopsis orchids do not produce more blooms from the same flower spike. Then I received a request from a reader to elaborate on that subject and explain my reasoning. Here I will do my best to do so.

I personally had never tried the sequential blooming method before because my main goal was to help the plants switch to growth mode as quickly as possible. My logic behind it was that the blooming process can be quite draining for the Phalaenopsis energy wise. Thus this may lead to fewer new leaves and roots produced during the vegetative period, and in time this may hinder the subsequent blooming seasons. So, I would always cut off the flower spike as soon as the flowers are completely dried off. I still think this is the best course of action for the sake of the health of the plant in the long run.

But if you wish to try sequential blooming (re-blooming from the same spike), here's what I would suggest you do.

First off, you need to keep an eye on the flower spike and check if it is still green or if it is starting to become yellow-brown and dry. If it is drying off, this may mean that the plant does not have enough strength to produce more blooms. In this case, just cut the spike off and try next year when the orchid will hopefully have more leaves, roots, and life force.

If the spike remains green, take a good look at the nodes where the flowers typically grow from. First, check the tip of the stalk. Does it look like a small green bud or was there a flower which had fallen off? If there is a bud, it may be viable for re-blooming. If not, the sequential blooming will not happen there.

the top hadn't bloomed

the top had bloomed

@Milky Green

Next, take a good look at the nodes down the spike. See where the last flower had been. The next node after it should be a "sleeping" bud covered with a thin sheath. These sleeping buds will be the source of our next re-blooming spike.

Here you have two options.

1. If the tip of the spike is green, leave the stalk as it is.
2. If the bud at the top already bloomed, cut the stalk between the last node which produced a flower and the first sleeping bud.

unavailable bud

"sleeping" bud

@Milky Green

Continue providing the same conditions for blooming (the temperature difference and the fertilizer). Hopefully, in time the orchid will start producing a secondary flower spike out of one of the sleeping nodes. Keeping my fingers crossed.

But be prepared that this may not necessarily happen or the new flower spike (and the new blooms respectively) will be much smaller.

Also, there is another possible outcome – the orchid may produce a keiki. The keiki is a small baby orchid which is an exact clone of the mother plant. This is one of the common ways that orchids reproduce themselves (more on this, in the chapter on propagation). Note that if you are dealing with a terminal spike (a flower spike which comes directly from the crown of the plant), there is a very high chance that the orchid will try to reproduce with a keiki, rather than re-bloom from the spike. This is a form of a survival mechanism when the plant is about to perish.

So, keep in mind the pros and cons of the sequential blooming and just see how your orchid reacts. Is the growth period postponed? Does your Phalaenopsis create fewer leaves and roots afterwards? Is the next blooming season weaker or did your orchid skip it altogether?

I believe that the whole process of growing plants is like parenting. We are getting acquainted with a different living creature, gathering data and experience, and eventually getting better and better at the process! I continue to learn new things about my plants every day, and tweaking my routines as I go. I think that's the beauty of caring for a live plant! We grow together.

WHAT TO DO AFTER
BLOOMING

*O*nce your orchid has finished blooming and all the flowers dry out and wither, it will (almost) immediately switch to growth mode. Here's how we can help it in this process.

First, cut off the flower spike (or spikes). I mentioned this in the re-potting section, but I will quickly remind you here as well – cut the stalk carefully at about 1 cm height or half an inch from the base. This helps the plant stop feeding the old flower spikes and start investing these valuable resources into the process of creating new leaves and roots right away!

Second, if this is a brand new plant, it is best to re-pot it with fresh soil and to perform a thorough root and leaf inspection. Go back and re-read these chapters, if necessary.

Third, continue watering and fertilizing as usual (following the instructions I gave you previously) and make sure you switch to plant food suitable for growth.

Here's a quick schematic to summarize the steps for taking care of your plant:

Variation I – you have a newly bought orchid which is currently blooming:

1. Place it at the correct spot (away from other plants in case there is a pest infestation or a disease);
2. If you notice any serious health issues, re-pot immediately and treat the problem as best as you can;
3. Follow a correct watering schedule;
4. Fertilize with food for blooming;
5. Remove the spike once the flowers dry out;

Note: if you are repotting a brand new orchid which comes with a bamboo stake (or a supporting stake made of any other natural material), it would be best to throw it away and grab a fresh one for the next blooming season. The bamboo stakes may become the perfect environment for mold, fungi or pests, and they may spoil your new potting medium. If the stake is plastic or metal, you can simply sterilize it with alcohol or hydrogen peroxide.

6. Re-pot and inspect the root system and the leaves (in case the plant was healthy);
7. Start fertilizing for growth;
8. Once the blooming season starts, create the necessary environment to stimulate the plant to create flowers;
9. Rinse and repeat – note that you do not have to re-pot your plant every year – once every two years is fine (if the plant is growing well and it is producing flowers).

Variation II – you have an old orchid which is not growing well and not blooming year after year:

1. Re-pot and inspect the root system and the leaves;
2. Place the plant in the correct spot – experiment and check how it reacts;
3. Create a tight watering schedule following the guidelines in the section on hydration;
4. Start fertilizing for growth;

5. Once the blooming season starts, create the necessary environment to stimulate the plant to create flowers;
6. If it does not, just continue taking care of your plant as usual – give it water and food and check whether it is growing well creating new large firm leaves and a good root system.
7. If it creates a flower spike, follow the above-mentioned instructions – fertilize for blooming and water regularly;
8. Remove the spike once the flowers dry out and switch to growth mode.

HOW AND WHEN TO PROPAGATE YOUR ORCHID

*T*here are several ways in which an orchid may be propagated. But in this chapter I will focus only on the simplest, safest, and most common way, in my opinion – the separation of basal keikis. A keiki (the term comes from the Hawaiian word for *"a child"* or *"an immature plant"*) is a baby flower which is an exact clone of the mother plant. There are two main types – flower spike and basal keikis. In the chapter on sequential blooming I briefly mentioned how a flower spike may actually produce a small baby orchid instead of a second blooming stem. This procedure often involves the help of a special growth hormone called cytokine which is found in cloning pastes (substances designed for stimulating the cloning of the orchid through flower spike keikis).

But since this is a Phalaenopsis guide for complete beginners, I will not go into the details of propagating your orchid in this method or even some of the more advanced ones (such as the flasking method). This chapter will deal with the most basic type which is more suitable for novices. This is the so called division of basal keikis.

In time, as orchids grow, they will create additional mini clones out of the main one – right at the base of the mother plant, hence the name basal keikis. This is normal and it is not absolutely necessary to divide them. Orchids do well in small spaces and if taken care of properly, they will continue to grow and bloom in one single pot.

I am personally growing "a triplet" in its original pot and with the proper watering and fertilizing schedule, it continues to grow and bloom. Actually, the two main plants create their own flower spikes and I am happy to enjoy them in a small space instead of having two separate pots on the window sill.

But let's say you wish to have two strong individual plants. And by strong I mean a secondary Phalaenopsis orchid which has at least three leaves and a root system which has multiple roots longer than 3 cm (1.1 inches). I personally like to wait until the keiki starts to produce its own blooms, just to be safe. This way I know for sure that the plant is strong enough to survive by itself. (*By the way, this is an awesome way to create a personal gift to a loved one who likes orchids.*)

Important note: *it is best to perform this procedure right after the blooming season is over. This way the new plant will have the whole growing season for itself to get over the shock of separation, to establish* *a powerful root system, and to develop as many new leaves as possible.*

So, let's see how we can divide these Siamese twins and propagate the main orchid into two separate plants.

The process is fairly simple and you will need just a couple of tools: a pair of gloves, a large container (for example, a washing basin or a tray), sharp gardening scissors, and strong nerves. :-D

The propagating procedure starts exactly like the one for a root inspection. Actually, this is the perfect opportunity to perform your regular root health check-up and pot soil change.

1. Soak the orchid in clean water for at least 15 minutes – just like you would do with regular watering;
2. Drain thoroughly and empty the pot in the large container;
3. Gently remove all the soil stuck to the roots, detangle the radicals, and disinfect them with hydrogen peroxide 3%;
4. Remove any rotten or dead roots and take a close look at the remaining root system;
5. Make an imaginary division between the two new plants and check whether each one of

them would have the necessary root system to survive the "surgery". Note that the roots have to be longer than 3 cm. (1.1 inches). The tips of the orchid roots are not able to absorb water and nutrients;

6. Carefully divide the plants by cutting the place where both orchids are joined. In my case, I didn't even need a pair gardening scissors – I firmly held both parts of the plant at their bases and divided them by gently tearing them apart. I must confess it was a little nerve-wrecking the first time around! :-D Of course, try not to harm any leaves or roots, although, I know it is not always possible not to cut or damage any healthy roots. That is why we need to have a strong well-developed root system before successfully propagating an orchid;

7. Disinfect the "wound" with the peroxide solution and place the new plants in individual pots with fresh soil as described in the section on re-potting;

8. Water them again with clean water, place them in an appropriate place in the recommended environment, and the only thing left is to pray that the "surgery" has been successful. :-D Let's keep faith in our orchids and rely on their sturdiness to survive any

type of stress! If I was able to do it from the first try, you can do it, too! Note that if the orchids had experienced a bit of shock from the separation, it is possible that they would develop a few new leaves which are smaller in size. In my case, the keikis I had separated formed one small leaf, and then they continued to grow normally afterwards.

ORCHID CARE DURING YOUR VACATION

*A*s you can see, orchids are not like the other house plants and you might feel a little anxious to leave them unattended during your annual summer vacation, for instance.

So, here in this section I will give you a few tips you can implement to preserve your orchid flower while you are away.

If you plan on being away during the cold months, your main concern would be the temperature drop the flower would experience. As stated previously, most Phalaenopsis plants feel comfortable at above 60° F (16° C). If you are confident the temperatures won't drop below this number for a long period of time, you don't need to worry about your orchid that much. For a short period of time, the plant could survive at temperatures between 50° F (10° C) and 59° F (15° C). In this case, my suggestion would be to check the root system for mold after you return. If present, treat the roots with the Hydrogen peroxide 3% as described in the section on re-potting and root inspection.

If you fear that the temperature drop would be severe and you are anxious to leave some sort of heating on, it is best to leave your plant with a relative, a friend or a neighbor to take care of it while you are away.

On the flip side, if you would be away during the hot summer days, your main concern would be dehydration and burnt leaves.

In this case, I would suggest you water your plant thoroughly before you leave, add some more water in the pot dish, and place the plant in a place away from sunlight. This will slow down the process of water evaporation, and the orchid can remain vital even for up to 10-15 days (depending on the room temperature).

Again, if you fear that this might not be enough, because the temperatures would be very high, you would not be able to supply any proper cooling, or you would be away for too long, just leave the plant with a friend along with simple guidelines (in case they are unexperienced with growing orchids).

That's it! That's all I have been doing while I am on my summer vacation and my orchids have been growing just fine! Remember that they are quite sturdy plants, and if you have been taking care of them properly, they will survive your trip and remain vital while you are away!

USEFUL TOOLS

*A*ll the necessary tools you need to grow your plant are compiled in this article and if you wish to get exact product suggestions, feel free to jump straight to the website.
Go to **https://bit.ly/2DB7rvb**
or scan the QR code:

Otherwise, you can use the information below to make your own personalized shopping list. Moreover, you can utilize it as a reminder of the most important parts when growing Phalaenopsis orchids (the item suggestions are accompanied with short summaries of the moth orchid care basics).

This list can also be a wonderful starting point for choosing a gift for a dear friend or a relative who loves orchids. If you know any avid Phalaenopsis fans around you, these orchid best purchases will help you figure out what to give them for any upcoming special occasion – a birthday celebration, Mother's day, Name day, anniversaries, Christmas, etc.

Orchid accessories for the best placement

The placement of your orchid is extremely important and it is definitely something which is often overlooked. Because at the core of the process of growing plants lies the effort to re-create their natural habitat as much as possible. And thus, the position of the flower will determine how much light it receives. Is there any wind current? Is it placed in an air conditioned room or not? You get the point. So, as far as lighting goes, here are a few options:

Flower lighting – in case the environment is too dark.

Usually, most orchid gardeners place their plant on the window sill for them to soak some natural light coming from the outside. But in some cases, this may not be enough or there might be too many plants and some of them have to be put in another location which is not very well lit. That is why getting such artificial source of light is a good idea for these scenarios. Maybe your home is facing North and there are high-rise buildings nearby and your place is not getting enough sunlight. Or maybe the cold winter months are too dark and foggy, and your plants are struggling with growth and blooming. Either way, the flower lamps might be a great choice to improve the environment for your precious Phalaenopsis orchids!

Textile blinds – in case there is too much direct light on the flower.

The opposite scenario is having too much direct light coming onto your beautiful moth orchids. This is not so good either. The natural habitats of the moon orchids are the Asian rainforests and most Phals grow under the partially sunny and partially shady spots under the trees. So, if your home is too bright and too hot, your beautiful plants might burn, get dehydrated, and perish. In this case, having textile blinds could be a wonderful solution! And I really like the Day Night types (and I have them, too, because my home is entirely South-facing) since we can pretty much create a similar mixed shade environment. These can be used whenever there is too much light coming straight to the orchids or only during the hot summer days, depending on the climate you live in.

A plant stand or a hanger – for better placement of your plants and more stability.

Most orchids are placed in mostly sunny places where there is a source of natural light coming in.

This is usually at the window sills and furniture near windows. Unfortunately, sometimes these spots are not available or they can be cluttered with other plants or home décor pieces. That is why you can consider getting a plant stand which would allow you to stack multiple orchids (or other flowers) in one place. This tool not only saves you space, but it also allows you to move it around and search for the best conditions for your precious plants. For instance, you may live in a hot and sunny area, and the amount of direct sunlight on your window sills may be too much for the Phalaenopsis which may end up burnt or dead. In such cases, consider placing your moon orchid somewhere inside the room away from direct sun rays. Another sensible reason for getting plant stands or wall/ceiling hangers is the risks of the plant toppling over. You may have noticed that orchids are very interesting and unique plants which often grow sideways (to prevent any excess water accumulating in the crown). This is all well and good, but more often than not, this may cause the center of mass to change and the pot may become unstable. One of the solutions is to place the planter in a more secure place, like a planter stand (with metal circles around the pot) or a pot hanger.

Thermometer and hygrometer – to check the most important elements of the environment.

As I mentioned in the chapter on placement, the temperature and the level of humidity are two extremely important parameters which will determine whether your orchid would be happy, alive, growing healthy, and blooming over and over again. So, it is always a good idea to check the temperature and the humidity of its environment. Remember that orchids are native to the rainforests of Asia and they feel comfortable between 60° F and 86° F (16° C to 30° C). As far as room humidity goes, it is advisable to keep it between 40% and 70%. If your climate is too dry, consider misting your plants with water often or adding a humidifier. It will definitely be of great benefit to your wellbeing as well. I personally have an aroma diffuser which serves double duty as a room humidifier. It has been great for battling dry air due to air conditioning.

Orchid supplies for proper watering

Watering orchids is probably one of the most controversial topics when it comes to growing these amazing exotic plants. Everyone has their own method and technique, but here in this section you will find some of the most essential products you would definitely need in this process. As far as my exact watering schedule goes, I do not think there is a one size fits all piece of advice in this area. That's simply because everyone lives in a different location with a different type of climate, and the conditions of the living space may vary greatly. For example, whether the space is air conditioned, how much light comes into the room, what the average temperature is, etc. Nevertheless, there are some ground rules I try to follow to determine whether it is time to water the moth orchids or if I should wait a little more. And if you are not exactly sure how to create your own personalized schedule, go back to the chapter on watering.

Wash basin or a bucket – choose a size according to the dimensions of the flower pot.

I know people have their own preferred ways of watering their moon orchids – some place them directly under the faucet and let the water run through the flower pot. Other folks pour some liquid underneath the orchid planter at all times and spray the airy roots from time to time. And these tactics are fine as long as they work for you. Nevertheless, my personal preferred way of hydrating my own

Phalaenopsis plants is by dipping them in a wash basin full of clean water for about 15 minutes. I also use this technique for fertilizing the plants with dissolved liquid nutrients in the water. That is how all the orchid medium can be fully soaked and retain most of the moisture for a longer period of time and revitalize the roots as well. By using this watering method it is of upmost importance to let all the excess liquid get out of the container so that the root system does not rot.

Spray bottles – it is best to get two separate bottles – one for watering the airy roots with clean water, and one for disinfecting the roots and the leaves. Remember to label them correctly and to store them away from children and pets!

The second important part of the watering process for Phalaenopsis orchids is hydrating the airy roots. They are as important as the "hidden" ones inside the pot. This is what's special about moth orchids – their ability to photosynthesize light using their root system. This gives them the ultimate back-up survival plan in case the leaves get damaged, rotten, or sick. That is why giving proper hydration to all the roots of the plant, including the ones which are sticking out of the planter, is extremely important. And also, let's not forget that the natural habitat of the moon orchid is the rainforests of Asia, so re-creating this environment as much as possible is crucial for their proper growth and blooming processes! In other words, use the spray bottle filled with clean water to spray onto the leaves and clean off any gathered dust or contaminations.

Labels – label your spray bottles and your plants. Another option is to buy self-adhesive paper and print your own labels. I also have prepared some examples at the end of the book you can use to tag your flowers and distinguish them when they are not in bloom.

Labeling may seem like a really insignificant task, but it is an absolute must, especially if you have a bottle or a container with a disinfecting liquid in it (such as hydrogen peroxide). You need to know which bottle is which and what it contains, so you or your family members won't make any bad mistakes. But labels also work great for the plants themselves. This is how you can keep track of your orchids and write down some important information – the date they were purchased, when they were last re-potted with brand new potting medium, what color are the blooms, etc. This is how you will know when it is time to re-pot your plant or inspect the root system (preferably every 2 years).

Water – it is best to use clean distilled water free from any impurities. Another great option I personally use is clean water purified with a *charcoal pitcher*.

Yes, Phalaenopsis orchids can be quite picky and demanding when it comes to their environment and all the nutrients we feed them with. And the first most vital part is watering. I know lots of people use simple tap water, and this could be perfectly fine in most cases. Unfortunately, sometimes this may not be enough or it could even be detrimental to the plant, especially if the water is extremely hard with lots of lime scale. This could build up on the root system and the leaves, impair the photosynthesis process, and block the absorption of nutrients from the medium. That is why I recommend you get the above-mentioned charcoal filter pitcher which would remove the lime scale as well as any excess Chlorine and other impurities.

Paper tissues – it is always a good idea to remove any excess water from the base of the flower to avoid rotting.

Let's not forget that the Phalaenopsis plants are usually located on trees with their leaves tilted a little bit to the side. This is not a coincidence! The natural evolution process forced orchids to grow this way so that excess rain water would slide away from the base of the plant. This is how the flowers are being watered without any liquid remaining which could cause any bacteria growth and rotting. Unfortunately, store-bought Phalaenopsis plants are usually facing straight up and the base of the flower may become the perfect hub for water, bacteria, and fungi, especially in the cold months when it is more difficult for the liquid to evaporate quickly. So, it is best to have some paper tissues at hand to gently remove any remaining water at the base of the orchid.

I will use this opportunity to gently remind you to avoid wiping the underside of the leaves where the stomata pores are located! For more information, go back to the chapter on watering.

Orchid tools for fertilizing

Universal (balanced) fertilizer – I am sure some orchid growers use this type of all-year-round plant food and have success with it. Its ratio is 20-20-20 (20% nitrogen, 20% phosphorus, 20% potassium). I personally do not use this type of orchid booster, and

I recommend using two separate types of fertilizer – one for growth and one for blooming.

Fertilizer for growth – you can grab a bottle of this liquid growth fertilizer for the main roots inside the pot and a spray bottle for the airy roots. This type of plant food is high in nitrogen and its exact ratio is the 30-10-10 (30% nitrogen, 10% phosphorus, and 10% potassium). Soak your Phalaenopsis plants with this solution (diluted in water as the manufacturer suggests) during the growth period of your plants – usually between March and September (in the Northern hemisphere). This essential part of the Phal's life starts right after its flowers wither and fall off the stem, and ends when a new spike is formed.

Fertilizer for blooming – again, your most commonly available options are liquid fertilizer for the main root system and a spray one for the airy roots outside the pot. This is a type of plant food which is high in phosphorus with the exact ratio of 10-30-20 (10% nitrogen, 30% phosphorus, and 20% potassium). As I mentioned previously, start feeding your Phalaenopsis orchids with this fertilizer once you see a brand new flower stalk starts to form (usually a mitten-like shaped stem between the last and the penultimate leaves). The typical blooming period starts around October and could last until March in the Northern hemisphere. You may have probably remembered that the most important condition is the temperature difference – this will determine when the flower spike will emerge (as long as the plant is healthy, strong, and "happy").

Orchid supplies for large and long-lasting blooms

Apart from the bloom-boosting fertilizer I mentioned previously, you will also need a few more things to make your beautiful Phalaenopsis orchid plant happy!

Support stakes – you can use simple eco-friendly bamboo stakes and clips (or plant wire) or metal ones with cage rings (these can be used without any clips).

The flower stalks of the moth orchid are quite strong and durable on their own, but we still need to secure them in some way or another. This will significantly improve their appearance (well, we get them mainly for their elegant aesthetic qualities, right?), and prevent the blossoms from bending forward. This could even change the plant's gravity point increasing the risk of it toppling over. Moreover, by keeping our Phal's flower stalk facing straight up, we would also avoid any potential accidents. Once I accidentally toppled my orchid by pulling the window curtain which clashed with the orchid's flower stem. Funny, right? Well, I wasn't so amused at that time! :-D So, definitely grab some cool stakes and secure your beautiful Phalaenopsis blossoms with some fixtures of your choice!

Just a quick reminder from the chapter on after-bloom care – remember to throw away any old supporting stakes made of natural materials (bamboo, wood, etc.). They may be plagued with mold, fungi or pests and thus ruin the fresh new potting medium.

Artificial Phalaenopsis flowers

The main reason why we are so obsessed with the Phalaenopsis orchids is their magnificently elegant aesthetics. Well, their blooms may be relatively long-lasting, but what do we do for the rest of the year during their growth season? One option is to leave the plants be as they are and enjoy their beautiful green foliage. But I would make another suggestion – you can definitely buy a couple of artificial moon orchid blooms and attach them to the plant as you would do with the real ones. This would still create a true royal-like or a SPA-like ambience to your home all-year long! And the artificial flowers are amazingly realistic and very difficult to distinguish the difference between them and the real thing! So, if you are very impatient for your magnificent Phals to start blooming, do not hesitate to upgrade your living space with these deco pieces!

Orchid must haves for successful re-potting

Gloves – always protect your skin against contaminations, fungi, bacteria, and pests.

As you may probably know, it is always a good choice to protect yourself while gardening, especially when it comes to caring for outdoor flowers. But even house plants can become contaminated in one way or another. So, it is best to keep your precious skin protected against any bacteria and fungi which are not native to our human microbiome. This is especially important when doing your regular re-potting process, and fertilizing. These procedures also involve using powerful chemicals which may irritate the derma, such as hydrogen peroxide or a strong undiluted liquid orchid fertilizer. So, always keep your hands safe with a fresh pair of gloves (consider getting a batch of eco-friendly compostable ones)! Oh, and of course – we should mention the aesthetic part of this situation – using such protection tools will keep your beautiful manicure intact and also you would avoid extreme skin chapping!

And one more important reason to use gloves when repotting or inspecting your plants – pests, mold, and diseases. As I mentioned in the chapter on repotting, using these protection tools is recommended in order for you to avoid transferring these health issues to your other plants at your home. So, if you are repotting a brand new orchid or you are dealing with a sick plant, make sure you use a fresh pair of protective gloves. After you are done with the flower, throw away the gloves or disinfect them thoroughly!

Hydrogen peroxide 3% - for disinfecting the roots and the leaves. The 6% solution is also an excellent option if you dilute it in the same amount of water.

Disinfecting is an extremely important part of the whole orchid care process. The Phalaenopsis plants may be quite sturdy and durable flowers, but they are certainly not immune to contaminations and infestations by malevolent bacteria, fungi, and bugs. So, it is best to protect the orchid right from the start by cleaning the whole root system and the leaves. I personally use hydrogen peroxide 3% since I believe that it is one of the safest and most effective options which do the job perfectly. But I know other gardeners use the stronger 6% solution or a completely different kind of disinfecting product. No matter what you choose, make sure you perform this procedure in the following situations:

➔ *right after you bring your Phalaenopsis plant from the store and all the flowers have withered;*
➔ *after it has been outside for a while;*
➔ *whenever you make a thorough inspection of your flower, in case there seems to be an issue with the roots or the leaves;*
➔ *every two years for prevention purposes. Also, make sure you wear your gloves from the previous orchid tool suggestion!*

Soil - you can use regular orchid soil or a variation fortified with fertilizer.

The so called orchid medium is probably one of the most important compounds you need for the proper care of your plant! This is their main source of nutrients and it has to be top notch! So, there are lots of options and different variations, but the most commonly used universal potting mix contains bark chips, coconut husk, sphagnum moss, cinder, etc. Keep in mind that some medium types have fertilizer added to the mix so that you can tweak your regular feeding schedule to be more sparse than usual. Also, it is important for the potting soil to be easily drained so that the root system of the orchid can "breathe" and to avoid root rotting. However, some types of media contain more sphagnum moss than usual which retains more water inside the pot. Keep this in mind when you create your watering schedule (follow the guidelines in the chapter on hydration to determine whether your orchid needs more or less frequent watering, rather than having a universal timetable).

Also, remember that previously I have mentioned that you can buy additional medium compounds to tweak your potting mix according to the environment of your home. For instance, if you live in an area with a continental climate where temperatures drop often, you may add more bark chips to improve the aeration of the root system and avoid the formation of mold. On the other hand, for hot and dry climates, adding more sphagnum moss may be sensible to lock more moisture inside the pot and prevent dehydration of the plant. Keep track of how your plants are growing and how they react to any changes of the potting medium. This process may need some tweaking at first until you notice that the orchids are happy on a regular basis.

Orchid pots – you can use regular plain orchid pots with plenty of holes, or more beautiful ceramic ones but with less visibility to the root system and less access to light (thus less photosynthesis).

When it comes to choosing suitable pots for your orchid plant, there is a wide variety of options. But here I will mention two of them which I think are appropriate for the proper growth and comfort of your flower. The first type is the regular and the simplest plastic ones – these are usually the kinds of containers which are transparent and flexible. These are excellent for complete Phalaenopsis gardening beginners since they provide the necessary light to the root system and can easily be accommodated with extra holes for even better aeration (if needed).

The second interesting type is the ceramic one. It is extremely beautiful and it is much more desirable for its elegant aesthetics. Unfortunately, there are a couple of downsides you need to take into account. The ceramic pots conceal most of the roots inside the container and do not allow extra light to be photosynthesized by the plant. And as we know, the moth orchid is among the plants known as epiphytes which use their powerful root system to additionally convert light into nutrients. Also, the ceramic pots make it a bit more difficult to determine whether your flower needs watering, and this is crucial when it comes to avoiding rotting of the radicals. As I mentioned previously in the chapter on the best placement of your orchids, to resolve this you can use regular transparent pots with lots of holes and slits for aeration, and inserting them inside larger ceramic ones. This setup is much more beautiful and adds much more stability to the plant as well.

Utility knife – for adding extra ventilation to the plastic pots, if needed.

Let's say that you already have a couple of Phalaenopsis orchids planted in some basic plastic pots. The store-bought plants usually come in such simple plastic planters without any additional holes (well, at least here where I live orchids are potted in such containers). If that's the case with your moth orchids, you certainly don't need to buy different kinds of planters, if you wish to keep these. But I highly recommend you use such utility knife to make some extra openings to increase the aeration of the root system. If during the cold months of the year the moisture inside the container lingers for too long and the risk of mold formation is high, you definitely would need to make this procedure or get some different kinds of pots equipped with more holes or slits.

Garden scissors – for cutting off flower spikes and dried/rotting roots and leaves.

This piece of orchid care equipment is extremely important for the proper gardening process of these magnificent flowers! The gardening scissors allow us to make the necessary cuts with extreme precision which is very important to the proper growth of the plant and for avoiding any damages. These essential orchid tools are extremely practical when you need to remove any dried leaves, rotten roots, or an old flower spike. Well, as far as cutting off the flower stem goes, I know there are different viewpoints on this. Some people leave their old spikes intact after the blooming season is over. In opposition, others prefer to remove them to boost the growth process of the plant by directing more nutrients and energy into the foliage and root development. Either way, you would still need to have a pair of these nifty cutting tools to use whenever necessary. And besides, very often store-bought orchids are not able to produce flowers from the same stem, and they dry out quickly after the blooming season is over. And so, you will have to cut it off eventually.

T-shaped flower tags – you can use these to write down all the necessary details of your plant - for example, the next re-potting date. You can also use adhesive printing paper to note some important info about your orchid – the variety, the color (to distinguish your plants during the growth period), the date it was purchased, etc.

Thank you!

I want to thank you for purchasing this book and reading it all the way to the end. I hope it has been helpful and informative. If you liked this volume, you can support my work and make it more visible for others who are looking for this kind of knowledge! I would deeply appreciate if you take a minute and write a short review on Amazon. I thank you in advance for your support!

Should you have questions, suggestions or success stories (fingers crossed!), you can send me a message at: **admin@mindbodyandspiritwellbeing.com**.

You can also find me on Facebook at: https://facebook.com/**iloveorchids2022**.

Looking forward to seeing your beautiful Phalaenopsis orchids!

Kind regards and best wishes,
Milky

Manufactured by Amazon.ca
Bolton, ON

39930359R00079